PRAISE FOR LOVE IN ACTION

This is book is a spectacularly profound, practical and simple guide for living through the heart and being of service. Well written with fitting anecdotes, this is a must read for those called to service in their life.

~

Such a wonderful inspiration! John Records gives us a journey of love and caring, and on the path of this book, helps us see the power of being in direct relationship with another who needs us...This book is highly recommended. Enjoy it!

~

I've been on a spiritual journey these last few years and found John's book to be one of the wonderful "roadmaps" that help guide me along. It's a practical resource on how to put love in action - wherever one is on their journey. Particularly liked the way he started with self love; for in accepting and loving ourselves we begin to develop our ability to spread the love and joy to others. The suggestion of using the Prayer of St. Francis for meditation was especially helpful; focusing ones heart and mind in a way that bears fruit when we go out from our quiet space to meet the world.

~

Love In Action came into my life at the right time. As a journalist, I've been fueled by anger and awareness of all that is wrong with the world around me. But I've come to realize that that is not enough. We can't run forever on negativity, as the present state of our nation and the world shows. This book sets out an approach that acknowledges the problems around us but does not require that I respond antagonistically.

∼

Beautiful in its brevity, this book gives you insight into how you can grow your understanding of why the world is the way that it is and what you can do to make it better, starting with yourself. It's filled with several short chapters/passages to inspire you. You can read through it very quickly and then return to it again and again at various points in your life.

∼

This is a beautiful short book written by a wonderful and wise man who walks his talk. If we could each embody even a fraction of the truths that ring throughout this book, it would go a long way toward healing our world. I am using each chapter as a morning meditation....great way to begin each day!

∼

John Records is a brilliant teacher, and in this book he eloquently shares insight into how to improve our daily lives, and strengthen our communities through love and kindness. Thank you John, for helping me to reach new levels of understanding about myself, and showing me how to share my gifts with others.

∼

Love in Action is a to-the-point guide for living a life in and of love, written in plain English. John provides the framework and path for bringing love into the world, through our very own lives. The implications that this have for living a full and rich life are endless. The book is broken down into short chapters that can be easily read in a few minutes each. A glance at the contents helps to quickly find the important or challenging aspects of life in that moment. In my own experience, practicing love in action benefits every aspect of my life, and supports a life with purpose. The true wealth of life is distilled in this little book. Thank you John!

LOVE IN ACTION

HEAL THE WORLD, HEAL YOURSELF

JOHN RECORDS

John Record
26 Feb 2018

Cover by

TERESA SHISHIM

Dedicated
To all who love, to all who serve

CONTENTS

PREFACE

~

My name is John. During 21 years building centers and programs to help homeless people in the Bay Area, I realized that love is the key element, and sometimes the missing ingredient, for helping people in need. I've found the same to be true while working in hospice supporting dying people and their families.

This lack of love pervades our society, and makes inevitable the overwhelming suffering described daily in the media, and the increasing hatred and lies that no longer are hidden in shame.

Love in Action is my response. This book distills what I've learned helping over 20,000 people, and through decades of spiritual practice.

As you read and reflect, you'll learn how to be more loving with your family, in the workplace, and as a volunteer. You'll learn about the simple spiritual practice of offering your entire being to love, and gradually being transformed into a vehicle for love's expression.

These lessons will help you to stay strong whatever comes your way, and to offer your love in action more and more to heal the world and yourself.

If *Love in Action* helps you, please share it with others so they too can benefit, as well as those they will help.

www.loveinactionbook.com has all the info you'll need.

Together we can touch thousands or even millions of lives.

With my best wishes and appreciation,

John Records
October 26, 2017
Paonia, Colorado

WHAT IS LOVE?

Love is to the spiritual world as gravity is to the material world: all pervading, holding us together, grounding, and reliable.

Love is connectedness, union, in which we see and respond to a person, creature, or situation in a deep and appropriate way, intuitively knowing what is best for all concerned.

Our love can expand to include all of creation, and the locus of our identity can shift so that we are not limited by our small sense of self, but feel the entire cosmos as our own being.

If we really see *any* person or creature, we love them. While we may tend to focus on those closest to us, for whom we may feel special responsibility and care, we can be open to loving all beings.

Loving them, we want to open our hearts to them and to share whatever we have that they might need, and to receive the same from them. Our love is not passive, but active. Love becomes love in action.

A LOT OF GOOD, YET

There's a lot of good in the world. Just visit a food bank or animal shelter (or better yet, volunteer there) if you want to see people at their best.

Yet despite the good in the world, we must acknowledge that our world is full of suffering. Just read the news if you doubt this.

The suffering is not just "elsewhere." I found it in my own community.

I was driving my old Volvo on a rainy, cold night and saw a man huddled at the side of the road, with his thumb out. I don't usually pick up hitchhikers, but the blasting warm air from the heater as the windshield wipers whipped back and forth reminded me of my good fortune. I wanted to share my comfort, so I pulled over and picked him up.

I opened the door and he climbed into the car. We shook hands and traded names. Joe said he needed a ride to the homeless shelter.

Once a well-to-do contractor, Joe had lost his home, his family, and his business. His lined face and his worn clothes told how hard his life was now. He spoke about living on the street – where to find work, food, and shelter.

Suddenly, I realized that Joe – the homeless person – was trying to instruct and help me – the middle class, employed person to whom such a thing as being homeless was unthinkable.

But Joe knew that anyone can lose their home, and that many are just a paycheck away from the street. So he told me what to do if the unthinkable should ever happen.

As Joe left the car at the shelter, I pondered his kindness and decided to follow him in. As the proverbial "fly on the wall" I watched as he spoke with the man at the check-in table.

"Can I get some dinner?"

"Gee, you're too late. We ate at the church tonight."

Joe's face fell. A withered man, sitting on a bench nearby, reached into his shirt pocket.

"Hey! I've got a hard-boiled egg you can have. How 'bout that?"

An *egg*. The carefully saved egg was a meal for a man who couldn't be sure he'd have enough to eat tomorrow. That egg was his savings account, his pension. It was all of his wealth. Never had I given anything as valuable as that egg.

This was love in action. The egg man's gift and service to his fellow human being inspired me to want to volunteer with the shelter, and that began over 20 years of passionate work for me, serving people without homes.

Really, you could stop reading right here. Just remember the egg man's answer to the suffering and despair right in front of him. He gave what he had to help another. He became love in action.

THE EASY WAY OUT

How do we respond to the suffering in the world, including in our own lives?

One solution is to turn away from it all, ignore it, and pretend it's not there. We can go numb and pursue our own pleasure.

This is the easy way out. Our culture offers many distractions to keep us cocooned from the pain all around us and within.

Yet it can be a blessing to really feel and acknowledge our own suffering and the suffering of others. It's a blessing because it means engaging with the truth of our lives.

BE THE CHANGE YOU WANT TO SEE
IN THE WORLD

Many religions suggest that the world's immense pain and injustice are acceptable somehow: there is a loving God whose ways we don't know but must trust; or that it's all an illusion; or that we're reaping the karma we've sown. Yet religions still encourage us to help those in need.

But suppose you don't have faith, and for you all of humanity's suffering is heartbreakingly, horribly real, and there's absolutely no sense to any of it. Then the blessing is that you still get to choose how you are going to live in the world.

You can change the world from one that is senselessly horrible to one in which there is compassion with your choice about how to live. You can choose that, to the extent of your ability, the people whose lives touch yours will be treated with love.

If you feel that the world is unloving, follow Gandhi's advice and be the change you want to see in the world.

ONE WORD IS WHISPERED

I love parables and stories from different times and traditions. Here is one of my favorites.

For every soul, there is an angel. The angel works with the soul before it is ready to take embodiment, before it is ready to be born into life on earth.

The angel talks with the soul about what to expect from life, and how to be ready for life on earth. And then, just before the soul is ready to be born, its angel whispers one word into its ear: Give.

In this one word, our angel tells us all we really need to know. Implicit in the angel's directive, give, is a way to heal the fragmentation of our lives, and to establish wholeness.

Service, love in action, is one expression of this giving. To give freely of ourselves, without regard to our own benefit, is love in action.

Only a life lived for others is worth living.

— ALBERT EINSTEIN

UNTIL OUR HEARTS ARE BROKEN

Until our hearts are broken, we're less-than-complete human beings. Perhaps sometimes we have to ignore the pain of others, just to function.

But if we're incapable of recognizing others' pain, then we're fragmented and cut off from ourselves. We all have the capacity to love and to care, but it has to develop, and that process usually involves some breaking, some pain.

The cold stone of our hearts is painfully excavated, which makes room for kindness to enter. Our hearts become a cup that overflows with love, and we enjoy a sense of connectedness with others.

ARE YOU WORTHY OF LOVE?

Our own suffering, including experiences in which we've been hurt by others (often while children) can cause us to feel unlovable and unworthy of love.

This feeling of unworthiness can limit our ability to lovingly support others. Moreover, even if we are able to support others, our own healing and ability to receive love is just as important as that of others.

Here is good medicine for you if you feel unworthy of love, in the form of a quote attributed to the Buddha:

Wherever you go, wherever you look, you'll never find anyone more worthy of love than you.

In a workshop I facilitated, we experimented with saying this to each other.

Wherever you go, wherever you look, you'll never find anyone more worthy of love than you.

What do *you* say? Is this true?

Wherever you go, wherever you look, you'll never find anyone more worthy of love than you.

Some in the workshop cried as they heard this, and some felt resistance to hearing it, not believing it to be true or even possible.

Wherever you go, wherever you look, you'll never find anyone more worthy of love than you.

There is no one more worthy of love than you.

Most seemed to feel that it's easier to tell this to someone than to hear it said to oneself.

Wherever you go, wherever you look, you'll never find anyone more worthy of love than you.

Why do we resist being told this? People in the workshop offered that many of us have had experiences as children in which we were taught that we are unworthy of love, bad, stupid.

It hurts to write this, as I think of all the needless pain adults cause children for a lifetime with such thoughtless and sometimes intentionally cruel statements. And yet,

There is no one more worthy of love than you.

In 1990, the columnist Sharon Salzberg discussed this with the Dalai Lama. Here's an excerpt from her essay:

"Your Holiness, what do you think about self-hatred?"

He looked at me seeming somewhat confused and asked in response: "What's that?"

... While I came to meditation at 18 as a result of dealing with feelings of inadequacy and self-judgment for my entire young adult life, the Dalai Lama didn't even know what the meaning of self-hatred was. When I explained to him what I meant by the term -- talking about the cycle of self-judgment, guilt, unproductive thought patterns -- he asked me, "How could you think of yourself that way?" and explained that we all have "Buddha nature."

LEARNING TO LOVE OURSELVES

How do we heal from these old wounds and self-hatred? If untreated these wounds persist into adulthood and can profoundly affect our happiness, and how we treat others and ourselves. Just hearing that "no one is more worthy of love than you" is not enough for many of us.

Through experiments in the workshop mentioned in the prior chapter, we found that *being physically touched while hearing this made it easier to hear and accept.*

Wherever you go, wherever you look, you'll never find anyone more worthy of love than you.

Even light touch helped, and that feels safer for people who have experienced abusive or harmful touching. We did this by working in pairs with each person extending an index finger so the finger tips of each person touched, then the statement "no one is more worthy of love than you" was offered. Wonderful, tearful, healing occurred.

You can try this for yourself, right now. Hug yourself and say:

Wherever you go, wherever you look, you'll never find anyone more worthy of love than you.

Or try it while touching another (use the fingertip method mentioned above), or have them touch you and say it.

Wherever you go, wherever you look, you'll never find anyone more worthy of love than you.

Often, we are told that meditation, which supports the realization of what the Dalai Lama calls our Buddha Nature, is the cure for all of our ailments. That may be, but my experience is that genuine, healthy connection with another human being can greatly support this realization. Therapy can help too, and can be based on this kind of healthy connection.

What happens when we learn to love ourselves? One of the workshop participants offered this poem:

> *The time will come*
> > *when, with elation*
> > *you will greet yourself arriving*
> > *at your own door, in your own mirror*
> > *and each will smile at the other's welcome,*
> > *and say, sit here. Eat.*
> > *You will love again the stranger who was yourself.*
> > *Give wine. Give bread. Give back your heart*
> > *to itself, to the stranger who has loved you*
> > *all your life, whom you ignored*
> > *for another, who knows you by heart.*
> > *Take down the love letters from the bookshelf,*
> > *the photographs, the desperate notes,*
> > *peel your own image from the mirror.*
> > *Sit. Feast on your life.*

— DEREK WALCOTT

Having learned to love ourselves, we can better love and serve others, and participate in healing the world.

TIKKUN OLAM

I f your heart is broken by suffering, you might participate in
tikkun olam, a Hebrew phrase that means, "mending the world."
The unity that can manifest and express in our own lives is
part of *tikkun olam*. We have the opportunity to increasingly,
consciously participate in mending the world. We start with
ourselves.

We mend ourselves through practices like meditation, prayer and
sometimes psychotherapy. In addition to our inner work, *tikkun olam*
is served when people come to together in love, service, respect and
mutual support. This can happen in the family, among neighbors, in
the workplace, and in spiritual communities, to name just a few.

Usually when we are engaged in loving service we don't think
about what's going on at a deeper level. We are probably immersed in
the needs of the moment, whether it be talking to a client, reading to a
child, or feeding a hungry person.

We are simply involved in the act, and that's a good thing; it's
better that we are not self-conscious, analyzing our motivation and
our response as we do these things.

But nonetheless, something is happening on a deeper level. People
invariably say that they feel good when they render service (and by

this I mean selfless service, in which we help to meet the need of another without seeking what's in it for us).

I think I know why we feel good when we offer selfless service. Suppose, for the sake of discussion, that there is something in which we live and move and have our being, and of which we are often unaware. I'd like to call it Spirit here; please use whatever words you like.

For the most part we don't remember our relationship to Spirit, but it feels good when we do feel more connected to it, and act and express ourselves in accordance with this connection. The great wisdom traditions encourage service as a path to connection with Spirit.

For example, Jesus tells us that he is present when we feed the hungry, give a drink to the thirsty, when a stranger is received into our homes, when we clothe the naked, when we take care of the sick. He tells us that by performing selfless service, by giving, we enter into connection with Spirit.

In St. Francis' famous prayer, he states, "It is in giving that we receive." It is not "in grabbing that we receive!" By giving, we keep making room for more receiving. Moreover, our capacity to give, and hence what we receive, increases with practice.

If we let our hearts open to the need of another being (or the needs of a situation), that will itself tell us what we must do, and how we must serve. For example, if our baby is crying we can decide to change the baby's diaper with love for our little one rather than with resentment over the task. By this simple change of attitude, responding to the baby's cry with love, we are drawn into alignment with Spirit.

More is going on than meets the eye when we participate in *tikkun olam*, mending the world. What was sundered in the Creation process is coming back together and being made whole again. It's our responsibility to be part of this, so that the world is mended in and through us. This is the path of love in action.

OFFER YOUR LIFE

You can heal your pain and help to mend the world if you offer your life in love and service. This is the bodhisattva way, as described in the prayer below from Shantideva, an 8th century Buddhist monk.

We might imperfectly live this way, but to even try to live like this aligns us with the power of love, which acts through us, supports us and develops us. Love can accomplish what we alone cannot, and presently we become love in action, love incarnate.

You may already be inclined to live in love and service. Shantideva's prayer might help you to do so even more:

May I become at all times, both now and forever
> *A protector of those without protection*
> *A guide for those who have lost their way*
> *A ship for those with oceans to cross*
> *A bridge for those with rivers to cross*
> *A sanctuary for those in danger*
> *A lamp for those without light*
> *A place of refuge for those who lack shelter*
> *And a servant to all in need*

For as long as space endures,
And for as long as living beings remain,
Until then may I, too, abide
To dispel the misery of the world.

Try saying this aloud, and see how it makes you feel. If it feels good, say it daily, and let this prayer guide your choices and behavior.

THE PRAYER OF ST. FRANCIS

The bodhisattva way is not exclusive to any faith or worldview. There are many contemporary bodhisattvas who have no belief system or code of conduct, whose lives are simple expressions of love. You don't have to adopt a belief system or bow to dogma to live this way.

That said, the prayer of St. Francis is a great example of the perspective of a Christian bodhisattva. However, some don't like the words "Lord" and "Divine Master". You can ignore them, or substitute words that work better for you--perhaps Higher Self, Great Mystery, or Spirit.

Here's the prayer:

Lord, make me an instrument of your peace
   Where there is hatred, let me sow love
   Where there is injury, pardon
   Where there is doubt, faith
   Where there is despair, hope
   Where there is darkness, light
   Where there is sadness, joy
   Oh Divine Master,

Grant that I may not so much seek
To be consoled as to console
To be understood as to understand
To be loved as to love
For it is in giving that we receive
It is in pardoning that we are pardoned
It is in dying (to our selfishness) that we are
Born to eternal life.

You can work with this prayer in three ways, described in the next chapters.

MEDITATION ON THE PRAYER OF ST. FRANCIS

The first way to work with the prayer of St. Francis comes from one of my teachers, Eknath Easwaran. He suggests that we memorize it and use it for meditation. This helps to internalize the words and even the consciousness of St. Francis.

Here are instructions in this practice, taken from the website of Easwaran's Blue Mountain Center of Meditation, www.bmcm.org.

In passage meditation, you concentrate on the words of an inspirational text or passage from one of the great wisdom traditions.

You start by choosing an inspirational passage [like the prayer of St. Francis] and memorizing it. The passage should be positive, practical and uplifting, and there are lots of passages you can choose from. Some are short, others longer, and they're from all different traditions.

Once you're ready with your passage, then

Sit in a chair, or on a cushion on the floor.

Sit upright and close your eyes.

Go through the words of your memorized passage slowly and silently in the mind.

Do your best to concentrate on the passage – when distractions come, just bring your mind back to the words.

At the end of the passage, go back to the beginning, or start a new one.
Do this for 30 minutes every morning.

If this attracts you, check out Easwaran's classic book *Meditation*, which provides more guidance on this way to meditate, and sets forth his eight-step program for spiritual development.

COUNTERACTING OUR OWN PAINFUL FEELINGS

The second way to work with the prayer of St. Francis is to use the stanzas literally. For instance, when we notice hatred in ourselves, the antidote is to feel love. It's a matter of catching ourselves in a thought or feeling, and counteracting that with the opposite.

So if we feel hatred for someone who harmed us, we might be able to find some love for that person as we think of the good things they have done for us or for others, and how they have been injured themselves and act in a hateful way because of that.

This doesn't mean condoning someone's harmful behavior, including our own. The point is to find a way to escape the trap of hatred, doubt, despair, darkness, or sadness. We can counteract this suffering by intentionally evoking the opposite feelings.

It helps to really consciously feel the painful emotion and how it expresses in your body. For instance, if I am feeling hatred and anger in my body, I notice tension in my shoulders and a sensation of being poorly connected to the ground. I might say to myself, "These are the feelings of anger and hatred I have toward whomever."

We're not suppressing the feeling or turning away from it, but rather welcoming it honestly and authentically. We are *not* pretending it isn't there. This immediately takes away some of its power, and can get us unstuck from the feeling.

Then, we can think of something good that the person did. In fairness, whatever they did or didn't do that has evoked our feeling, there is more to them than just that. So, having acknowledged our feeling, we take the antidote of appreciating something the person did that evokes a positive feeling like love.

When the feeling of hatred (and its partner anger) is met with the feeling of love, we can feel a shift into a more neutral place, not caught in hatred or love. We can apply this practice to all the painful emotions listed in Francis' prayer. What a relief!

STRATEGIES FOR SUPPORTING OTHERS

T he third way to work with the prayer of St. Francis is to apply the stanzas when we notice negative thoughts and actions in others. As an example, if someone is full of despair, it might be possible for us to support him or her in finding hope.

I'm not suggesting a mindlessly Pollyanna approach, nor swooping in for a quick fix when someone's life has been shattered. Rather, genuinely listening to a person in despair is in itself healing and provides hope, for it demonstrates that they are not alone, and that someone cares about them. At the right time, it may be possible to offer other forms of tangible support.

To people in pain, we can be the tangible expression of the positive qualities mentioned in the prayer of St. Francis: love, faith, hope, light and joy. Offering ourselves in this way gradually transforms us more and more into the living expression of love.

THE SECOND STANZA

So far we've just looked at the first stanza of the prayer of St. Francis. Here's the second stanza:

Oh Divine Master,
> *Grant that I may not so much seek*
> *To be consoled as to console*
> *To be understood as to understand*
> *To be loved as to love.*

Again, if you don't care for "Divine Master" feel free to substitute words more to your liking.

The orientation here is clear: we're not seeking the benefits of consolation, understanding and love for ourselves, but rather are offering these to others. The purpose is to get us out of our seemingly endless cultivation of self-centeredness that, in extreme cases, leads us to try to reshape the entire world to serve our sometimes infantile neediness.

There *are* times that we need and want consolation, understanding and love. If we are living the prayer of St. Francis, these will generally come to us without having to seek them.

FRUIT FOR YOU

Without trying to attain a benefit for ourselves, simply by living the prayer of St. Francis in accord with the first two stanzas, we can enjoy marvelous fruit.

For it is in giving that we receive
 It is in pardoning that we are pardoned
 It is in dying (to our selfishness) that we are
 Born to eternal life.
What goes around, comes around.

As you sow, so shall you reap.

We get back what we give, and in my experience much more than that.

When we are able to pardon (forgive) others, we greatly heal our own pain.

When we let go of our striving to benefit ourselves, when we die to our selfishness, we enter into the timeless freedom that is called "eternal life" in the prayer.

Tikkun olam: as we mend the world, we mend ourselves.

LET LOVE BE OUR COMPASS

Let love be our compass. One way we experience the ground of being, Spirit, is as love. The subjective feeling of love arises when Spirit is active in us. Action that comes out of that love, that stirring of Spirit, is service, compassion, kindness, and healthy connection.

So love is a reliable compass, and when we act guided by love we bring more love and harmony to the world. Conversely, if we are in hate rather than love, we are increasing the fragmentation of the world.

If we are aligned with Spirit, if we are full of love, then that acts through us, motivates us, and expresses in blessing and action in the world. This includes the normal activities of our daily lives – our work (particularly if not harmful to others), and our relationships with family, friends, and colleagues.

For most kinds of service we can imagine, a machine could perform the task. For example, a vending machine can provide hot stew to a customer. But a crucial ingredient is missing, and that ingredient is, of course, love.

The Talmud says, "The whole worth of a kind deed is the love that inspires it." This underscores that service of the kind discussed in this book is not merely a mechanical act. Rather, as Sarah Patton Boyle, a U.S. civil rights activist, said, "Service...is love in action, love made flesh; service is the body, the incarnation of love. Love is the impetus, service the act, and creativity the result with many byproducts."

When Patton Boyle says, "Love is the impetus," we see again the tug of Spirit inviting us to participate in the flow. The pull of love, its invitation to us, can take many forms: a sense of connection with someone in need, the inspiration to give something we have just because somebody else might need it, the desire to help someone who's in a situation that sparks a memory of some old pain or a loss of our own.

The "many byproducts" Ms. Boyle mentions are diverse and unpredictable; they range from a warm glowing feeling in the giver and receiver to the utter transformation of either or both, and perhaps even of those around them.

OFFERING OURSELVES INTO THE
WOUNDED WORLD

A young friend said to me, "I'm trying to figure out what to do with my life. Do you have any thoughts on this?" I pondered as we walked through a beautiful park, just strolling and chatting.

Knowing that my friend pushes herself pretty hard, I said, "Well, I'd give a different answer to a different person. But my answer for you is to first give yourself permission to have fun."

"But I can't do that," she said, "when the world is in such trouble. People are starving. A war is looming. And women and children are being abused every day. How can you tell me to have a good time?"

"I just want you to be able to enjoy yourself," I said, "even though there is a lot of pain in the world. We've both seen grim, desperate, fearful activists who feel driven and angry, and who are doing their level best to save something that they see as hanging by a thread. I myself have been like that. I don't know how effective we really are when we're coming from that place. We're running on a corrosive fuel that doesn't feed us and that in fact eats away at us and those around us."

I continued, "I'm not putting people like that down--they have the guts to confront what they see is wrong. And it's true that terrible things are always going on. But it's also true that there is always cause for joy and for celebration. We have to find some kind of accommodation between the wounds and the joy of our world. I think that to the extent our engagement with the wounds of the world can come from our joy and strength, we will be more effective than if we come from the place of desperation and fear."

I concluded by urging her to root herself in what she finds to be true, good and loving, to have a positive vision of the future, and to engage the world from that place. I'm happy to report that she has found a way to do this, most of the time.

BE LIKE A BIRD

The balancing act between the wonder and wounds of our world is expressed beautifully by the women's singing group Libana in its song, "Be Like a Bird," based on Victor Hugo's "Wings." As Libana puts it:

Be like a bird, who pausing in her flight
on a limb too slight,
feels it give way beneath her,
yet sings, sings, knowing she has wings;
yet sings, sings, knowing she has wings.

We can take the risk of alighting on the ever-unreliable branches of the world, engaging with the pain and fragmentation, because we know that our wings will bear us up until we choose to alight again.

The wounds, the various kinds of pain and suffering that we see in the world, are manifestations of our disconnectedness from Spirit; they are part of the way we experience ourselves as separate from other beings, other creatures, and from the world itself. It is important to understand that the wounds of the world are our own wounds.

HEALING OURSELVES, HEALING THE WORLD

I f we open ourselves to the wounds we see in the world, if we let our hearts be broken by it so that we *must* act, we become love in action. We accept the invitation to participate in the healing of the wounds of the world, which are our own wounds.

This is the healing of ourselves. By the same token, the joy of the world is our own joy, and is not different from ourselves. We can rejoice in the triumphs of others, and surf on the waves of their happiness.

I emphasize the wounds more than the joy because the wounds are more frightening and challenging to connect with. Opening to joy generally is easier!

But as Spirit expresses itself more fully in our fragmented world-view, as we offer ourselves in service to the wounds of the world, a healing occurs that encompasses us as well as those we serve.

For instance, if we are inspired to help a woman who has been abused, that within us which responds to her need is part of her need, part of the world's wound which she and we suffer together. The recognition of her suffering, along with the effort and intention to help heal it, are part and parcel of the healing itself. And as her personal healing begins, the universal wound is also addressed.

As a corollary, beginning to heal ourselves, making ourselves more whole, bringing ourselves into alignment with Spirit, enjoying our lives and expressing and developing our gifts--all this helps to heal the wounds of the world. Another way to say this is that our individual blossoming and our natural healthy, joyous expression are part of the world's healing.

LOVE IN ACTION IN THE FAMILY

One of the easiest places to offer love in action is in our families and in our friendships by putting others' needs ahead of our desires. Opportunities to do this may arise at unexpected times.

For example, a friend returned from work and was sitting on the couch reviewing the day's mail. Her 18-year-old daughter came to sit by her and she put the mail down, turning her attention to the young woman. "You know, Mom," she said, "I really appreciate it that you're ready for me whenever I'm ready for you. There's never been a time that I needed you that you weren't there for me."

In this case, it was a simple, natural thing for the mother to drop what she was doing to be present for her daughter. It's good to take advantage of these opportunities when we can.

Eventually, we go our separate ways. We are wise to provide love and support in the moment, and not put it off for another time that may never come.

LOVE IN ACTION AT WORK

"I can't be servile. I give service. There is a difference."

— DOLORES DANTE, U.S. WAITRESS AS QUOTED IN
WORKING, BOOK 5, BY STUDS TERKEL (1973)

We can picture "tiers" of love in action outside the family. Someone might progress from having a regular, off-the-shelf job, to doing such a job with a loving and serviceful attitude, to volunteering now and then in an environment overtly dedicated to service, to having a job that's completely dedicated to love in action.

In some ways it's much easier working in a helping profession, because we don't have to struggle to make room for real love in action and we get a lot of support in living and behaving this way. For most of us, full-time employment in a recognized service profession is hard to come by, so our work-a-day job becomes our primary arena for love in action.

Offering love in action is possible in any context or environment. Whether we are working in a homeless shelter or in a tech company, whether we are reading to the neighbors' kids or volunteering at the hospice, we can offer love in action to the people and the work at hand.

VOLUNTEERING

"We make a living by what we get, but we make a life by what we give."

— WINSTON CHURCHILL

I know many people who live out love in action in the business world, but they also sometimes seem worn out when their work environments are dollar-driven and dehumanizing. They tell me that volunteering is refreshing and revitalizing.

Take for example the viewpoint of Jim, a real estate broker who volunteered in a homeless shelter:

To me this place is an oasis. Here I can get fulfilled. It's an island in the middle of this turmoil that I can find refuge in. This is real for me and I treasure it. I talk it up all the time. It is an oasis for me. And when I go in there, the staff and volunteers are concerned about me and I'm concerned about them. It's a nice, nice feeling.

As volunteers, we should take small steps and have patience. Look at all the residents, all the people who are homeless, look for that personal pure essence. And have no expectations, none.

If you get involved you'll be happier and you'll be more fulfilled than in anything you've ever done. It won't make you rich in material things, but it'll make you wealthy in friends, relationships and personal well-being. You'll go to bed every night and you'll say, 'That was a good day. That was a cool day today.'

You won't have that plaque on the wall for being the outstanding car salesman or whatever, but you'll have it in your head. And you'll sleep well. The inner joy you get is great. You'll find all those other important things will still get done but they won't be as big a deal any more. They're just not that important.

CELESTE

There are many challenges in offering love in action, in offering ourselves into the wounds of the world. Now and then we encounter something we aren't ready for.

Some years ago in my work in homeless services, I met a mother whom I'll call Yvonne, and her 10 year-old daughter whom I'll call Celeste. (These are not their real names.) Yvonne was worn by her years on the street. She was used up, but not yet disposed of by our uncaring culture.

Yvonne lived with her daughter Celeste in the nooks and crannies of our community, in the homeless shelter when possible, in the back of an old car when she had one, in the bushes when she didn't.

Celeste was someone special. At age 10 she was years behind in school (when she had the opportunity to attend), trusting enough to be always ready to laugh, with an expectant sweetness behind her usually hesitant and puzzled eyes.

I had daughters a little younger than Celeste, and that opened me to her. Thinking of their brightness and competence, appreciating how they were ensconced in our happy family life, I sadly watched Celeste at the shelter.

Seeing her trusting sweetness and the unlikelihood of her life being a happy one, I reached out to her, and Celeste and I made a deep connection. When I saw her in the shelter, I was able to use my Daddy-of-daughters skills to elicit a special smile from her, letting her know that I knew who she was and that I liked her.

After about a month, it was time for Celeste and Yvonne to leave the shelter, and I lost track of their whereabouts after about year. Many years later, Celeste and Yvonne appeared again in our community. I was told that Yvonne's boyfriend had been pimping Celeste, selling her on the street.

The image of Celeste as a clouded, innocent child dominated my inner vision and I was torn to pieces. I sobbed, unable to bear the thought of her being repeatedly molested by harsh men, her trust broken again and again and again.

In the course of a phone discussion with a clergy member about an unrelated matter, I mentioned my anguish and asked him to pray for me. "Of course," he said. "And wouldn't you like to pray together for her, too?"

I had never thought of that. My response to Celeste's situation was all about me, although it purported to be about her. I was wrapped up in my vicarious agony and somehow it wasn't about Celeste any more; it was about me and my response to a world in which this could happen to an innocent, and by implication to my own daughters.

RISK THE BROKEN HEART

We may be afraid to love and help people in need because we don't want our hearts broken.

This is a natural feeling, but when we allow our hearts to break, we also open ourselves to a powerful force that can transform our own lives. We realize that we must help. And then we find a way to help.

If we don't work with people and creatures in need, then who will do it? We really have no alternative but to courageously face the pain in the world, a world in which thousands of children die daily from preventable causes.

We must risk the broken heart, embrace the pain, ask for help, rest when needed, and never give up. To turn away in order to protect our own comfort is to reject the call to participate in the healing of those in need, as well as our own healing, and the world's.

OUR RESPONSIBILITY IS LIMITED

In addition to the risk of heartbreak, to really become love in action is to risk feeling overwhelmed. How can we prevent nuclear war, house all of the homeless, feed all of the hungry, heal all of the sick? If we can't help all of those in need, if we can't cure the problem, then the temptation, the cop-out, is to do nothing.

Mother Teresa had good answers for that one.

Never worry about numbers. Help one person at a time, and always start with the person nearest you.

If you can't feed a hundred people, then feed just one.

Our responsibility is limited. All we have to do is make ourselves available, show up, and do our best. To remind me of this, I've had these signs on the wall of my office:

Full effort is full victory.

— GANDHI

Don't feel totally, absolutely, irrevocably responsible for everything. That's my job.

— GOD

Offering love and help in this spirit, just showing up and doing our best, realizing that the outcome is not in our hands, makes it easier. When it feels hard, when we have feelings of desperation, fear, or even pride, we have temporarily lost our way, and have become focused on ourselves.

When loving service feels hard and challenging, we can find our way again by opening ourselves to the needs of the people and the situation in which we're offering service, thus re-establishing the connection that is part of the healing. We can also engage in other practices that support deep connection, such as meditation and prayer.

If we can face the challenges of service, overcome our fear, dare to love, dare to alight on the branches that we know will give way beneath us, we will share Mother Teresa's experience:

I have found the paradox that if I love until it hurts, then there is no hurt, but only more love.

What we give, we receive; we are healing ourselves as we heal the world and its wounded.

DIFFICULT PEOPLE AND SITUATIONS

Sometimes when we are offering love in action, we encounter difficult and even demeaning situations.

Books and courses are offered on how to deal with difficult people, and I won't dwell on this subject here, except to mention that, in such situations, we must keep in mind the wounds we all share, just by being human beings.

When we remember this fundamental reality, we try to be patient with unpleasant or inappropriate behavior and we try to help others regain their balance and perspective, setting boundaries as needed so that we feel our integrity is preserved.

You don't have to be a doormat or to accept abuse, and yet we are less prone to be concerned about this if love has taken us over. We might see only the beauty of any wounded human being, despite their external and inner wounds.

When love has taken us over we don't need to *try* to be patient with other people. The aspect of our character that gets impatient, annoyed or frustrated is deactivated when love has its way with us.

ENABLING

There can be an artful balance between providing loving support and enabling harmful behavior. If we are acting under the influence of love, most likely we will do the right thing.

When my head comes into the picture along with my loving heart, I find it useful to keep in mind what I'm trying to accomplish, which usually is to help someone to feel cared about, respected and supported as they take their next steps, without encouraging dependency.

As an example, if someone on the street asks me for money to buy food, I might say, "Let's have a meal together instead. My treat." Sometimes the person will reject this because he wanted the money, not the food.

Pope Francis suggests a different approach. As reported in the New York Times (March 3, 2017), the Pope says give money to panhandlers and don't worry about it.

But what if the money is used to buy a glass of wine? If "a glass of wine is the only happiness he has in life, that's O.K. Instead, ask yourself, what do you do on the sly? What 'happiness' do you seek in secret?"

According to the Times, the Pope said:

...the way of giving is as important as the gift. You should not simply drop a bill into a cup and walk away. You must stop, look the person in the eyes, and touch his or her hands. The reason is to preserve dignity, to see another person not as a pathology or a social condition, but as a human, with a life whose value is equal to your own.

I think I understand and appreciate the Pope's perspective. We agree that such an encounter is an opportunity to engage with genuine, nonjudgmental love and respect, and that it's better to give freely than to turn away. There is a transformational opportunity for both parties if there is genuine connection.

Yet I think it's also important to assess whether our intended help is really a good thing for the person. We should not use this concern as an excuse to turn away from the person.

The desire to provide genuine help may require us to understand at a deep level why the person needs help and to address root causes. If we strive to really connect with those in need and to provide life-changing support, our lives may be transformed. This was my path to over 20 years working with homeless people, which was one of the great blessings of my life.

MISTAKES ARE INEVITABLE

Because of our imperfect humanity, mistakes are inevitable. We might be doing our best for someone close to us and find that, despite our loving intentions, we have failed to meet their needs, or even worse have hurt them.

Speaking from experience, I can say that this feels horrible. However, we all have our own baggage, wounds and blind spots that can undermine our relationships, and we are not in control of how people respond to us.

Sometimes there is no apparent way to reconcile conflict, to heal misunderstandings. In these times, the best we can do is to:

- act with loving kindness
- realize that not everyone will recognize our good intentions
- accept that we will make mistakes and do our best to learn from them
- correct our mistakes when possible
- find whatever help may be available to support reconciliation
- recognize that we each have our own work to do, and that

painful interactions may lead to growth and healing for all
concerned
- keep in mind that our lives and struggles are held and
supported by an awakening Love that is bigger than any
person, and trust that this Love will eventually heal all
suffering.

My own practice of love in action is imperfect and I stumble more often than I like. I imagine it's like that for you, too. It's ok to stumble, and important to get back up and try again.

PARTING WAYS

Sometimes we need to part ways with others whom we have loved.

We might learn that a relationship is not good for us, or for another person. Or there may have been loving connection in a relationship at one time, and that may have faded.

If and when the time comes to part, we can do our best to do so lovingly. Too, even though we may part in this life, we do remain connected at a deeper level, and united in the oneness of Spirit.

THE BODHISATTVA WAY

I've had the unimaginable blessing of knowing and being loved by a fully developed bodhisattva, my teacher Paramahamsa Hariharananda. Through a lifetime of service and meditation, he became a luminous incarnation of Love. Just to be in his presence was uplifting. His example shows that this growth is possible for us, too.

If you dare to love fully with a broken heart, you might open and grow more and more until you become an inexhaustible treasure as described in this prayer.

May I be the doctor and the medicine
And may I be the nurse
For all sick beings in the world
Until everyone is healed
To clear away the pain of thirst and hunger
And during the aeon of famine
May I myself change into food and drink.
May I become an inexhaustible treasure
For those who are poor and destitute;

May I turn into all things they could need
And may these be placed close beside them.

— -SHANTIDEVA, GUIDE TO THE BODHISATTVA'S WAY
OF LIFE

BEING IN LOVE

Often, we think of "being in love" as head over heels infatuation.

Here, I'm offering "being in love" as a state of consciousness in which love--without an object-- pervades our awareness. And if there is no object, no particular beloved, there also may not be a subject: we may dissolve into the love.

St. Paul wrote about being in love in this way, when he said:

Love is patient and kind
    Love is not jealous or boastful
    It is not arrogant or rude
    Love does not insist on its own way
    It is not irritable or resentful
    It rejoices not in the wrong, but in the right

    ...

    Love bears all things
    Believes all things
    Hopes all things
    Endures all things
    Love never ends

These are the qualities expressed when we become Love. It's not that we're trying to behave in this way, but that Love has overtaken us and the expression of these qualities is the most natural thing for us.

BECOMING LOVE

We can become Love, or perhaps it's more accurate to say that Love can become us.

We might not become Love for all beings all of the time, but initially at least for some people and creatures some of the time we represent Love in their lives.

We learn to enter into and be transformed by this love a little at a time, often first with our immediate family. If we say "yes" to greater opportunities to love, the family we love will grow to include all that is. Love will consume our smaller constricted sense of self and we will dissolve into Love.

The path is simply to offer all of yourself to Love. To paraphrase St. Teresa of Avila:

> *Love has no body but yours,*
> *No hands, no feet on earth but yours,*
> *Yours are the eyes with which Love looks*
> *Compassion on this world.*
> *Yours are the feet with which Love walks to do good,*
> *Yours are the hands with which Love blesses all the world.*
> *Yours are the hands, yours are the feet,*

Yours are the eyes, you are Love's body.
Love has no body but yours,
No hands, no feet on earth but yours,
Yours are the eyes with which Love looks
compassion on this world.

A tremendously powerful spiritual practice is to offer in service to Love your eyes, your ears, your mouth, your mind, your heart, your hands, your feet...and more.

Here's an example of offering oneself in service to Love, from my own practice:

I sit in a quiet place where I won't be disturbed.

Then I exhale deeply several times with an audible sigh. This helps me to let go of whatever may be on my mind.

I rest in the stillness that I feel at the end of the final exhalation. There's no hurry, so I take my time and really feel the stillness.

Looking at my hands, I say "I offer my hands in the service of Love."

Touching the top of my head, I say "I offer my mind in the service of Love."

Going slowly, I continue touching various parts of my body (eyes, ears, nose, mouth, heart, belly, legs, feet) offering those in service of Love and feeling the body part as I say the words.

I might sit a bit and bask in Love. Then I get up and let Love move my hands, and then let Love move my entire body through swaying as I stand or through walking. This provides practice in letting Love live in and act through my life.

The important thing is to invite Love to take over your life, and to be the living channel for and expression of this Love. Become Love in Action.

THANKS AND REQUEST

T hanks very much for reading *Love in Action*. The world needs what you have to give. May you stay strong, and offer your special gifts with love to those in need.

If *Love in Action* makes any difference in your life, please share it with others.

Reviews are very helpful. I'd love it if you would go to www.loveinactionbook.com for easy links to leave a review, and to share with others.

With appreciation,
John Records

ACKNOWLEDGMENTS

~

Thanks to Glena Records for reading drafts, and commenting on cover designs.

Thanks to Teresa Shishim for the cover.

Portions of *Love in Action* appeared in my book *Invitation to Service: Stories from COTS.*

ABOUT THE AUTHOR

~

John Records is a reformed lawyer turned nonprofit leader, spiritual teacher and transformational coach. He lives on the side of a mountain in rural Colorado, with no traffic lights within 30 miles.

www.moltengoldenmountain.com
john.records@gmail.com